THE PERSON vs. THE PROCESS

THE PERSON vs. THE PROCESS
JACQUELEEN M. BIDO, EDD

For information contact:
Bidioism LLC
Email: ceo@bidoism.com
Website: www.bidoism.com
Book and Cover design by Jacqueleen Bido

ISBN: 979-8-9898904-7-7

First Edition: January 7, 2024

Table of Content

DEDICATION

To my beloved children

Cristina, Alecc, Aleccia, Mackaiyah, and Mackennah

may you always remember how mommy kept her word.

The **#wholeteamwinning**

ACKNOWLEDGEMENTS

I want to thank first and foremost God for manifesting in me the words to present in this book. I want to thank my grandmothers, Dinorah Estecumber and Guillermina Alvarado, whose resilience to succeed in America has been the leadership model I had the privilege of witnessing first hand as a Latina in America. To my Mother Anna Colon, my sister Kathleen Morales, my brother's Cesar C. Bido JR., Carlos Bido, Sergio Bido, and Felix Bido, I thank you for supporting me through it all. To my 4 nephews Xavier (Javier), Cesar Bido II, Trevor, and Matteo, Auntie loves you.

To my Father Cesar Confesor Bido ``El Gran Bido'' who is with me in spirit at all times… I thank you because in life you always pushed me to do anything I set my mind to. "CONCENTRATE"! You would say. This book is one of the many things I told you I would do in your lifetime but who knew you would go so soon. In the end I continue to complete the list of things I told you in my lifetime knowing that you would be proud.

To Elizabeth "Delacruz" Turner, thank you for holding me to my word.

To Dr. Andrea Osei, thank you for holding me to my word.

To Joel Flores, thank you for holding me to my word.

#WHOLETEAMWINNING

BIDOISM:

1. A philosophy to provide "A Strategy for Peace of Mind" and "Authenticity.

INTRODUCTION

There is something about working for a person with particular ways and actions that can scar you even after you no longer work for them. Moreover, if you aren't mindful, you too will exhibit the same behaviors. There is a profound dichotomy between those who take negative experiences and refuse to repeat the behavior onto others vs those whose pain has served as an indoctrination of the negativity they will perpetuate onto those around them throughout their career. This has been the essence of many work environments and relational experiences that are the catalyst to positive or negative mental health in and out of work settings. While positive or negative can be relative depending on the situation or person one thing is for sure negative experiences will not sustain a positive or successful culture over time.

If I knew then what I know now it wouldn't have made a difference without the proper application of the knowledge. From large to small corporations, to small mom and pop local businesses, to grassroots organizations there are expected outcomes that drive their existence, success and overall sustainability. When these outcomes are not met two things happen in most cases:

1. People seek to blame something or someone for the outcome

or

2. People seek to find the solution for the reason or reasons something occurred whether it was as a result of something or someone

What the most successful leaders know is that blame in and of itself only perpetuates more failure if not coupled with a solution or a request for one. What you will find within the pages of this book are the solutions, experiences, and intentional strategies that elite leaders understand about the essence of "human nature" and inevitably the impact human nature and the processes implemented have on successfully achieving any goal.

Please Note: The following test is essential for your understanding of the contents written within these pages.

1. Get a piece of paper or write on the blank page in the book, put the pen or pencil in your hand and on the piece of paper draw a circle.

2. Now draw a long line.

3. Now draw a short line.

4. Now draw another short line.

5. Now draw another short line.

6. Lastly, draw a final short line.

Now that you have completed that look on the next page to see what I expected you to draw.

This is what I wanted and expected you to draw.

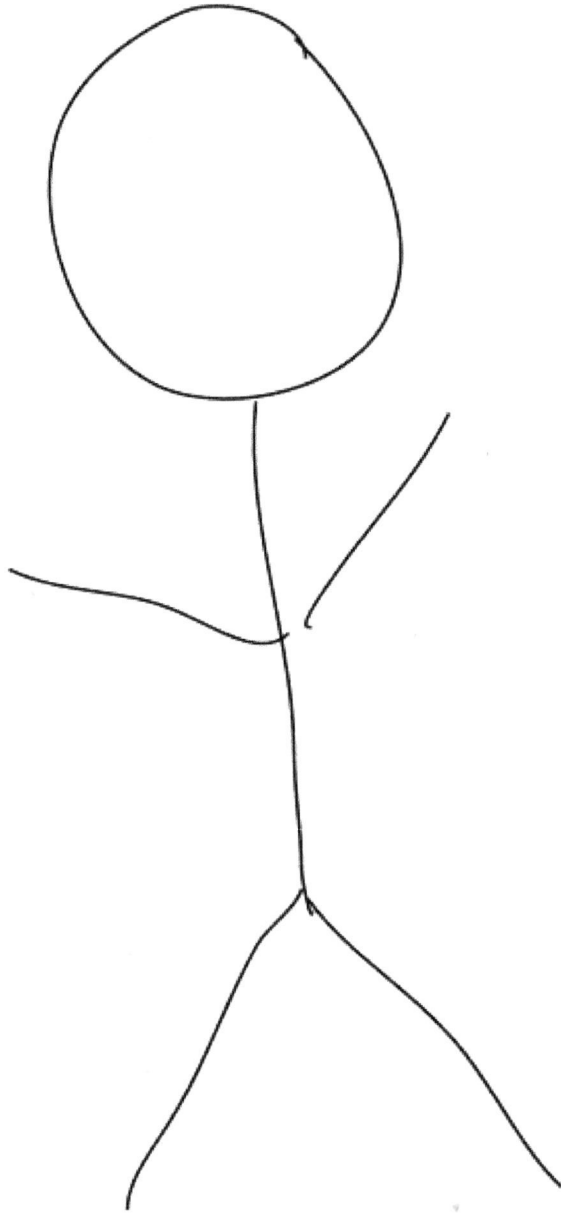

These are some of the drawings that people came up with:

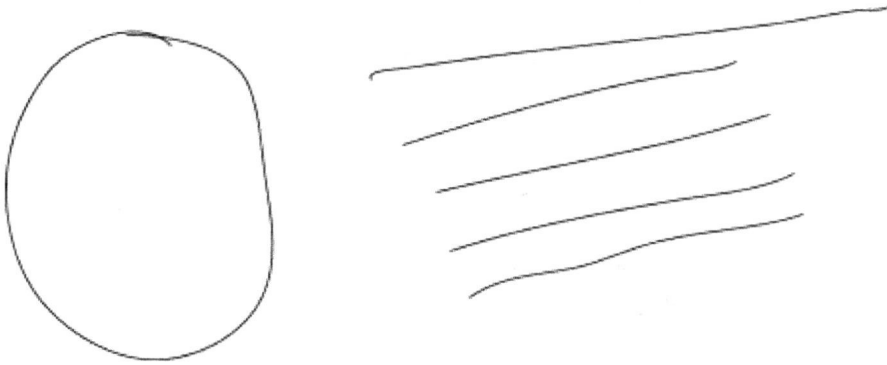

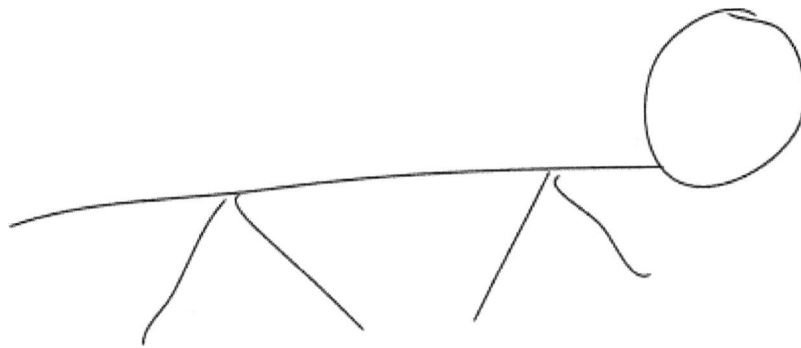

Reflect and answer the following questions:

Did you draw the same thing as I did?

What should I perceive about you as a leader if it is the same?

What should I perceive about you as a leader if it is not the same?

Next, observe and analyze some of the outcomes of people you may have never met. What do you perceive about them as leaders?

Is there something I could have done to drive the outcome to be the same?

What do you perceive about the person?

And

What do you perceive about the process?

This book is written in a way that is aligned to this quote from Dr. David Hawkins in his book...

"This book is devoted to the process of making the simple obvious"

- Dr. Dvid Hawkins

As you delve into the contents written within the pages of this book make sure you take the time to reflect on what is being stated and how it relates or doesn't to the person you are and the process(es) you engage in both professionally and personally. Some of your reflections will be prompted intentionally via the questions you are posed throughout your reading and others will happen naturally as you analyze what is being proposed.

Above all…

You must be ready to receive this knowledge.

Are you ready?

If yes, continue reading. If not, ask yourself why? And then continue reading.

PART I

"The best time to plant a tree was 20 years ago. The second best time is now."

—- Chinese Proverb

CHAPTER ONE: CITE

A Leader knows the work... even if they don't do it!

-Bidoism

Leaders Know The Work

There is an epidemic plaguing the work environment and it is due to individuals in management positions not knowing "The Work". The Work is defined in this book as a sequence of task(s) with a predetermined outcome that is expected upon completion of the task or tasks. In order for "The Work" to be completed a leader should be able to establish or request a sequence of steps to get the work done and more importantly to understand what the work is. Though how the work is done may vary from business to business and employee to employee the steps should give both the leader or employee a sequence of actions that lead to an intended positive result.

Often when under the guise of "Limited Experience Leaders", employees are expected to perform "The Work" with little to know guidance nor a clear understanding of the expectation. This is preempted by a "Get it done mentality" yet there is no clear understanding of what "done" is. The employees subsequently go about their day feeling lost and under led, second guessing their initial thoughts about how to do the work, and a host of other negative emotions that impact the results. When the leader or those tasked with leading don't know "The Work" it is a breeding ground for blame when success isn't produced, cultivates professional resentment and an undesirable work culture.

As Steven Covey stated in the 8th Habit,

> "The problem is , managers today are still applying the Industrial age control model to knowledge workers." According to Covey, when you treat people like things it insults and alienates them, depersonalizes work, and creates low-trust, unionized, litigious cultures."

The reason this book was written is because of the lessons I learned while coaching and managing people in various leadership and non-leadership roles. Even more so due to the toxic people who were charged to lead yet, disgraced the very essence of their capacity due to lack of leadership acumen. I found that there was a continuous struggle that proliferated the work environment and affected efficiency and the people who worked there at every level of leadership. These issues were not just isolated to small businesses but inclusive of large corporations. In fact, the effects of attrition affected large companies in compartmentalized ways dependent upon who was "leading" the department. In order to address these effects I coined the phrase "The Person vs The Process". The following chapters will provide the ways in which The Person vs The Process Methodology can change how you lead.

Under this methodology you will be introduced to the **CUREIS Lifecycle: Cite, Understand, Reflect, Empower, Implement, Survey**. The contents within these pages will empower you and those you lead with the strategy for sustainment of a culture of efficiency, a reduction in attrition, and a true understanding of elite leadership through the clear development of goals, intended outcomes and the implementation of authentic professional development and empowerment. The difference between other leadership books and The Person vs The Process is that this book was developed in alignment with the BIDOISM Philosophy at its foundation to provide "A Strategy for Peace of Mind " and "Authenticity. It is at its core a solution to the stressors of leadership, employment, and it offers a new approach to an old problem. If you are open to the reality of the existence of elite leadership then this book is for you.

But wait... You may be asking yourself "Why did I even develop The Person vs The Process Methodology?"

Well, it was born out of being tired of observing toxic leadership, toxic work environments and ultimately poor performance. The more leadership responsibilities the more I saw the gaps in the system and depending on my organizational authority in some instances there was nothing I could do other than inform those above my authority who I perceived would, could, and should do something about it. On my level and below I made sure to empower those around me, created resources like Standard Operating Procedures (SOP's) for myself and others, as well as advocate for the reform of the policy inequalities that existed within the matrix.

As I was coaching others to lead in order to address the systemic gaps within their business or organization for every problem or concern cited I would ask these two questions:

Is it the Person? or is it the Process?

Immediately they would ask "Can it be both? and my answer was always the same:

"In situations where you perceive it to be both the person and the process
always go assess the process first then the person."

Throughout this journey I want the reader to take a holistic approach at leadership, overall management, and the work they are tasked to see to success. This book is geared towards leaders in large corporations, departments, or small business owners starting or growing their businesses to the very employees aspiring to evolve into leadership roles. Throughout this book you will explore techniques that will assist in leadership, training, and decision making, all while achieving the intended outcome. If you are a person aspiring to lead or be successful in your position the methods explained in this book can be applied from your personal lens as an employee and assist in helping you perform on a leadership level no matter what your title is. The reader of this book is someone who seeks to find solutions to work challenges and cultivates a culture that emanates integrity and ethics of profession. This book is for current and aspiring administrators, leaders, business owners or employees who want to become Elite Leaders. This book will change how you lead and most of all how you look at challenging situations both professional and personal. What would you pay for peace of mind? The cost of this book, consulting, one-to-one coaching,... you decide!

The Price of Excellence

"We are what we repeatedly do. Excellence then, is not an act, but a habit."

– Aristotle, Greek philosopher

If I gave you a dollar for everytime you were in an environment that understood the "Price of Excellence " how many dollars would you have? Some people would have none. As a person when you understand the price of excellence you also understand that it comes with sacrifice. Excellence takes time, Excellence takes discipline, and Excellence is ultimately a way of life. Yet, the very people who understand that in theory do not understand that when it comes to the work environment or in Leadership. In some instances excellence is the expectation with little to no evidence that the person hired to do a given task has ever been excellent in anything. But furthermore excellence has not been defined. Excellence is defined by Merriam Webster as the quality of being outstanding or extremely good.

As a leader have you ever been "Excellent" at a specific thing? How long did it take? And What did you have to sacrifice to become Excellent?

Many times we work for institutions that expect excellence without a definition of what it looks like, a surface level definition of excellence and worse not a single example of excellence to reference within the company matrix. Excellence comes from the knowledge of the work you are tasked to do and the implementation of the steps that lead to success.

10,000 Hours to Excellence

I read a book titled The Outliers: The Story of Success by journalist and author Malcolm Gladwell. In his book, Gladwell dives into what makes the most successful people so good at what they do and discovers the commonalities they have which provided them with opportunities to succeed. Upon reading this book it prompted me to reflect on "10,000 Hours". Like literally what have I ever done in my life for 10,000 hours that has made me "Excellent"? A couple of things came to mind but more importantly I realized that in leadership we must take the time to identify the things that have made us "Excellent" in order to model, explain and teach to others. All of my leadership expertise was earned and had to transcend institutional racism and sexism throughout my career. Not only could I cite the 10,000 hours I also understood that my excellence could and did open doors for others who looked like me. Does your excellence open doors for others? In "Elite Leadership" to be excellent it has to.

As I continued to analyze the writings of Malcolm Gladwell he codified in his work some of the following points:

#1 Success is the compilation of lots of factors
Gladwell presents the concept that individual success is the result of multiple factors mingling and mixing together to form a perfect storm of circumstance and talent.

There is a point where your hard work meets opportunity. In further reflection on this concept I found that it is the awareness of your excellence and tallents aligned with the awareness of what opportunity looks like at different stages of your career that leads to success. There were many times just to get into a specific corporation I took an entry level job to then transition internally to other positions that suited my qualifications. This strategy enabled me the opportunity to acquire the knowledge I needed while surpassing the online resume abyss for positions that were being internally placed for existing employees. It allowed for the ability to network with different people to glean other opportunities that would lead to many positions of leadership. I didn't let my excellence in any area cloud my ability to see the pathway in.

#2 10,000 Hours

Gladwell reiterates the common idea that you need 10,000 hours of experience with something before you can become an expert in that field. This is not only an anecdote passed down between cultures but also scientifically valid according to Gladwell.

The first thing I did when Gladwell affirmed the number of hours to be "10,000" I broke that down into time increments that were realistic to my life. The following is what I found:

10,000 hrs divided by 8 hrs a day = 1,250 days

and

1,250 days divided by 365 days = 3.4 years

Then I broke it down again

10,000 hrs divided by 4 hrs a day = 2,500 days

and

2,500 days divided by 365 days = 6.8 years

And a one last time:

10,000 hrs divided by 2 hrs a day = 5,000 days

and

5,000 days divided by 365 days = 13.6 years

This additional breakdown of the 10,000 hours provided me the ability to analyze how I had spent my time and would spend my time. For some, 13.6 years seems like a long time but for others 13.6 years of consistency coupled with intentionality has been the essence of their success. If 10,000 hours is the number then how do we use that in leading others within their career growth. When do they implement the 10,000 hours? Do we recruit employees with this in mind? If the answer is no, why don't we? Even more profound is as a lifelong learner and educator if 10,000 hours is the foundation producing excellence how dont we integrate this into the matrix of Academia? By the time a student graduates they could be "Excellent" at something.

I noted the following point specifically because I don't agree this applies:

#3 Success is Partially Based on Luck

In order to obtain the number of hours necessary to become an expert and in order to have a culture that nurtures your interests, you must be incredibly lucky compared to everyone. These are the titular "outliers": those who were born at the right place and the right time to have an interest that led them to riches and greatness and the culture and aptitude to pursue their expertise to its conclusion.

In my experience "Luck" doesn't exist in leadership, especially as a person of color. Ask any person of color if they were lucky to be in the position they were in and if they answered "Yes" I would love to know how they defined "Luck". If I had to depend on luck I wouldn't be where I am today. Luck doesn't exist when you are brought up within institutional racism. You work for everything you have in leadership and are consistently made to prove your excellence, authority, expertise and merit. That isn't luck, that's resilience to transcend beyond the inequities within many work environments. Thus, it is imperative that our excellence as leaders creates avenues for career growth for those who come after us so they do not have to face similar gaps in the existence of inequitable policies that perpetuate toxic work environments.

#4 Practical Intelligence

He made a distinction between two types of intelligence: practical and analytical. The latter is what is tested by IQ exams and is what normally is prized by society. But practical intelligence, otherwise known as street smarts, is also important for those who want to become successful. Having a lot of practical intelligence will help you avoid social blunders and help you maximize social opportunities.

There is something to be said about intelligence and that is being intelligent and the application of intelligence are emphatically different in impact. There are leaders who will promote based on analytical aptitude but fail to assess the necessity for the practical application of intelligence. As a leader we must look at the person from dual lenses which allows for the impact of leadership to transcend beyond words to form real-time results which is important in utilizing the person vs the process.

#5 Opportunity is Exponential

Earning your initial successes and opportunities is much more difficult compared to once you have some achievements under your belt.

The achievement of success feels arduous at times because as humans we rarely take the time to plan out the steps that are right before us to attain initial success. I didn't become successful in my own career until I outlined for myself what I thought success was. I defined the initial steps I needed to take explicitly. In the age of technology you have the access at your fingertips to begin outlining the steps to where you want to go as a person and as a leader. The key though for me was seeing beyond the first milestone of success but rather the success point after. For example, when I was entrenched in assignments in the middle of the ocean while on active duty in the navy in order to obtain my associates I was already looking at my bachelors program. The same thing with my Masters all the way to my Doctorate Degree. It was the process I needed to see just so that I could solidify even my first step in enrolling in school. The opportunities that came from achieving my first academic goal were a catalyst to being able to engage in the opportunities I have today. How have your initial steps solidified where you are today?

#6 Talent Matters

Although the 10,000 hours mentioned earlier are the key to becoming an expert in any field, everyone must also understand that you have to have some natural aptitude to become a success in any field or ability.

When it comes to talent all leaders should understand that the natural aptitude for something may be blocked by the necessity of circumstance. There are times when a person merely takes a position because they had to. They don't align naturally with any of the work but Life has spoken louder than any task you could give them as employment. Thus, you may see that talent is masked by the stressors of life. Some people in leadership positions may never take the time to dig a little deeper to find out how they can support that person in navigating the positions they have been called to do nor do they take the time to show them the pathways to growth and opportunity. The talent that exists can be lost because we haven't taken the time to cite the person's capabilities.

#7 Fulfillment

Gladwell speaks of three main factors that your work or vocation must give you in order to feel fulfilled in your life: autonomy, complex enough to provide you with an adequate physical or mental challenge, clear connection between your efforts and any possible rewards.

From any capacity, fulfillment is imperative for sustainability. In leadership roles fulfillment is even more important because when you are not fulfilled as a leader your decisions and behaviors can result in the very reason attrition occurs in work environments. You are the very reason that the process fails because you are not able to lead as a result of your own misery. Leaders and everyone must be mindful of this within the person vs the process because if you are not fulfilled you will implement the wrong solutions.

The Cost of Attrition (COA)

Cost-of-attrition (COA) is the cost your organization incurs when an employee quits or is fired. It can vary based on the role, salary, skillset, and seniority of the employee. It can include the loss of productivity, morale, knowledge, and the expense of recruiting, onboarding, and training a replacement. It can range from 16% to 213% of annual salary depending on the industry and the position. It can have a significant impact on the economy, the state, the city, and the local community.

The Impacts of COA

The magnitude of COA can fluctuate depending on factors such as the employee's position, salary, skillset, and level of seniority. These costs encompass various aspects, including:

1. **Productivity Loss:** When an employee departs, there is a temporary decline in productivity due to the need for knowledge transfer, training of a replacement, and the adjustment period for the new employee.

2. **Morale Impact:** High attrition rates can negatively affect the morale of remaining employees. Disengagement and demotivation may result, impacting overall team dynamics.

3. **Knowledge Drain:** Departing employees take with them valuable institutional knowledge, expertise, and insights. This loss can hinder organizational efficiency and decision-making.

4. **Recruitment and Onboarding Costs:** Hiring a replacement involves expenses related to recruitment, interviews, background checks, and onboarding. These costs contribute to COA.

5. **Training and Development:** Organizations invest in employee development. When an employee leaves, the investment made in their training becomes a sunk cost.

6. **Administrative Expenses:** Processing paperwork, conducting exit interviews, and managing benefits administration add to the overall cost.

7. **Impact on Projects and Deliverables:** If the departing employee was working on critical projects, their absence may delay deliverables or disrupt project timelines.

8. **Reputation and Brand Image:** High attrition rates can harm an organization's reputation, affecting its ability to attract top talent and retain clients.

Every leader should know and understand the Cost-of-attrition (COA) at every level of leadership within the scope of their own responsibilities. This is in direct alignment with implementing the Person vs The Process methodology. Understanding what it takes for a person to do the work successfully will support the decrease in workplace attrition. Imagine for a moment if the salary of leadership was impacted by the percentage of attrition? Would leadership look different? The following stories will provide a snapshot of work environments that exist that either promote the decrease of attrition or the increase of attrition. As you read them, reflect on whether there are similar examples in your own journey and on what you would have done as a leader in the scenario.

A Tale of Two Trainers

Training is one of the most important things in a work environment. It allows for individuals on any level of employment to learn and grow in their capacity. Yet there is a tale of two trainers that I must bring to the forefront especially when implementing the methodology of The Person vs The Process.

> **Trainer 1**: Trainer 1 is a supervisor in the department. They have been there for some time and were called upon to train their staff on the process which would educate them on how managers conduct evaluations. This training was offered in order to build the capacity of staff members as there were positions available that would call upon anyone who applied to know how to conduct managerial evaluations as one of the requirements. While all staff members would not go for the available opportunity the Director wanted to ensure that they did everything to ensure their staff were qualified to do that specific requirement. In addition, by educating the staff on the process they would know exactly how they were being evaluated by the managers in the organization. The

Supervisor conducted the training and the staff received a certificate as evidence of what they have learned.

Trainer 2: Trainer 2 is an employee that has been at the company for some time. Throughout their employment they have had the aspiration for moving up in the department. The employee has always received gleaming reviews and evaluations from all the administration they have worked for. The employee has all the required credentials to become manager. A managerial position was advertised for the department the employee worked in. The employee decided it was the right time to apply because the job description coupled with their experience over the years were a perfect fit. Time passed and the position closed but the employee was not hired. The employee kept working diligently and thoroughly as always though disappointed didn't let it affect how they did the work they were accountable for. Monday came and the Supervisor approached the employee and said "I would like you to meet the new manager. They came from out of state. I would like for you to train our newly hired manager this week." Trainer 2 the employee did what the Supervisor had requested. On that very Friday, the employee submitted their 2 week notice that they would be leaving the job they had done for the past 10 years.

What did you observe in the examples of Trainer 1 and Trainer 2? Of the trainers what was your perception of them based on the information provided? What positive process did you identify in the example? What areas of growth did you identify in the example? In each scenario provided answer was it "The Person" or "The Process" that led to the outcome.

The reasons these examples were provided is because some of us can relate to

Trainer 1 and Trainer 2. For Trainer 1, I recall many times having effective leadership in place that would ensure all of the staff were trained in areas for capacity building, personal growth, and overall leadership best-practices so that we would be prepared for promotion. This was offered to everyone whether they stayed with the company or went on to other endeavors. We were allowed to crosstrain with other employees on our level and above our positions authority so that we didn't work in silos. This enabled the department to function and support one another in an employee's absence.

When it comes to Trainer 2, I have met quite a number of people personally who have been overlooked by their Supervisors and Department Heads when it came to promotion but yet were the ones that had to train the new hire. In most cases the new person was hired for the very position they had applied for. Over 75 percent of those individuals who shared that similar experience ended up leaving their job on their own. They articulated feelings of hurt, anger, disbelief, and utter insult when they would then be asked to train their incoming boss. In addition, they identified the fact that in their jobs there were little pathways to leadership.

When it comes to utilizing employees for training there are a few things a leader should keep in mind:

1. The trainer should be a supervisor or leader within the department. If an employee is selected to conduct the training or being groomed for leadership the supervisor should still introduce the employee and manage the expectations of the other employees and participants.

2. Leadership programs should be formally packaged and made available to employees. Even if there are no guarantees made for future employment the formal presentation of the program will be key for engagement.

3. Rarely if ever should an employee train someone for the position they applied for and did not receive. In order to limit the need for this one

should cross train laterally and or have specific employees trained in various aspects of the department.

4. Implement a formal training department or person who develops "Standard Operating Procedures (SOP's) which provides guidance for how each part of the process is conducted.

5. Create training videos that employees can develop and reference in the future. This allows for independent learning outside of face-to-face interactions.

As you continue to read, some of the aforementioned practices will be explained in greater detail as when it comes to The Process they are essential in creating an environment of equity, efficiency and empowerment.

The Double Up

"Please, find a desk or bring one from the other class room". I can recall this day vividly as it was the 4th time in a week, 12th time in a month, and who knows how many times in a year that due to teacher absenteeism, lack of substitutes, and overall low recruitment of teachers in the district I was doubled up in my classroom with 46 students for yet another period. One would think that by the 8th time there would be a solution put in place that would not impact student learning to this degree. In addition, it would immediately bring into question whether this was the career for me. From discipline to increased pressure to meet district standards with little resources I pondered daily "why was I still here?" I decided to reach out to the administration and I quickly understood that it was bigger than them. What I was experiencing, others were feeling the same pressure to achieve with little to no direction. Independent solutions to problems were often met with disciplinary conversations that started with "due to district policy we aren't able to (fill in the blank)" to most of the possible solutions for the high attrition of teachers. I began to ask myself, is this just our district or everywhere? As time progressed the limited resources and support led to me leaving teaching as a career choice completely.

The Dichotomy Between Resources and Resourcefulness

The ability to be resourceful should not be the commonplace of any work environment. Resources should be present in order to ensure the employee or employees have what they need to be successful in their position. Resources that are tangible, accessible, or acquired. They can be available daily, as needed, or in emergency situations applied immediately without direction or authority. Too often organizational structures are built on the premise of employees being resourceful with little resources. This can lead to employees feeling stress where there shouldn't be. It also impacts productivity in ways that even successful outcomes cannot compensate for the time it took to achieve had the resources been present to begin with.

Understanding the importance of resources within a process is necessary. Often employees are evaluated for outcomes that have not been sustained with the resources for them to be successful. If an employee is required to meet a sales quota but has not been provided the training necessary to understand the very product they are selling it can be the impetus for the gaps in productivity. If an employee is required to bake a certain number of cupcakes in 8 hours but there aren't enough ovens to meet the baking requirement for that output then they will not succeed. If that employee is then evaluated on the number of cupcakes they have baked that would not be ethical or conducive to a positive work environment. This is due to the fact that the employee cannot be resourceful about the lack of ovens without the autonomy to do so or the resources to do so.

An employee can be resourceful if the request was to increase the number of community partners that can partner with the business. They can use their own

network of community knowledge to do so. They can be resourceful and google
a list of local businesses and organizations. They can host a meet and greet and
invite the community to learn more about what the business does. This is just
one example of an employee being resourceful. If the aforementioned employee
is evaluated they essentially had the autonomy to implement resourcefulness to
be successful when in the ladder example they could not. In the person vs the
process when it come to evaluation one should remember the difference
between "resource" and "resourcefulness":

Resource: a stock or supply of money, materials, staff, and other assets
that can be drawn on by a person or organization in order to function
effectively

Resourcefulness: the ability to find quick and clever ways to overcome
difficulties

Or

Resource = Things

Resourcefulness = The use of things

When people are being held accountable to a specific outcome we as leaders
should be realistic about what resources are needed to be successful at
minimum. If their resources are truly limited then the employee should be
trained on the most effective way to succeed with limited resources in the
process. We as leaders should not leave to chance what we have control of. Each
employee should be provided best-practices they can employ in order to be
successful. If we do not provide these essential resources and the process calls
for these resources to be in place for consistent sustainable success then we
must question to what level we judge the performance of those hired. To be
blinded to the necessities of the resources needed for success is to guarantee
the indoctrination of a culture that begins to doubt their very own employment
decisions. In addition, we cultivate an environment that breeds burnout because

resourcefulness is not sustainable over time. The perception of value is then measured by the leadership's inability to provide the resources to be successful. The academic field is one that consistently feels the impact of such expectations.

The Pathway to Opportunity

Does your organization have a pathway to opportunity and growth? Laying out career growth for those you lead is pivotal in creating a culture of growth. This allows for individuals to see a path to success equivalent to the process they implement everyday to meet the mission of their role, the department and over all the organization.

The Morning Breakthrough

It was 4 am and my alarm clock went off as usual. The commute to my job on public transportation was one that if I even missed the first bus I would for surely be late to work. My job was definitely a necessity and it kept the lights on, food on the table, and a roof over my head. I felt that with my limited education I needed to stay where I was. Though there were growth opportunities in the workplace I didn't know how to go about it. I went into work, did my allotted hours and came home until one day this interaction changed my lens on my career and the opportunities around me. As a result of my commute I would get to work 30 minutes before my start time. I would sit in the break room and read my book of choice and drink my coffee. Early one Monday morning one of my supervisors approached me and asked "Would you be interested in becoming a manager?" I immediately looked around to make sure the supervisor was talking to me. Never did I even think I could be a manager but once the supervisor told me that there was a career growth program at the job that mentors employees through the process of leadership it made me feel empowered. I applied for that program and now in my 10th year of leadership I remember what that supervisor did for me and make it a point to expose my employees to the opportunities that exist for them.

"Widen the path of opportunities and continue to leave a powerful and positive legacy in this world."

-Luis Fonsi

The Indoctrination of Toxicity

"Toxic Leadership" is a word that immediately makes me think of the term "oxymoron". How can something toxic be coupled with leadership? For some work environments "Toxic Leadership" was the essence of daily interactions. As the boss hovered over my shoulder as I clicked on every button it was clear that I was in a highly micromanaged environment. After every click she would ask "why did I do it that way?" No Matter what I answered her reply was "well the better way to do it is like this? At first I was taken aback because it was my first day and had never been trained in their process. I didn't make a big deal about it and just used my own previous experience to get me through the daily work expectations. Unfortunately, day in and day out the boss would continue the same behavior. One day I asked "Is there a day where we can go through the process of the work so I can do it as you would like." The response was, "I don't have the time to train you." Each day I would do the work as best as I could with little support. The time for my evaluation came and there was no area she saw me as successful. The entire meeting was degrading as every correction was followed by if I were doing it I would have done this or I would have done that. What she didn't know is that I was tracking my productivity daily. For every section of my evaluation I could cite and support the evidence of my work. After that day, I began making plans to exit the position. The day I gave her my 2-weeks notice I felt bad because I knew if she didn't change her approach I wouldn't be the last qualified person she would lose.

"Moral autonomy appears when the mind regards as necessary an ideal that is independent of all external pressures."

- Jean Piaget

The Autonomy of Decision Making

In many coaching sessions when I am reviewing evaluations or written warnings of employees I often ask this extremely important question:

> **Was the employee given the autonomy to do it without permission?**
>
> Or as stated in resourcefulness
>
> **Was the employee given the autonomy to be "RESOURCEFUL"?!**

This question sometimes baffles the leaders I coach as I am often asked "What do mean?". What I mean is was the employee explicitly told that they could make that decision, one that is out of their scope of responsibility without clearing it with management?

> **Autonomy** -self-directing freedom and especially moral independence
>
> **Authority** -power to influence or command thought, opinion, or behavior; freedom granted by one in authority

In both definitions we observe the use of the work "Freedom".

> **Freedom** -the absence of necessity, coercion, or constraint in choice or action

The words that stand out here are "choice or action".

I have seen so many times when a person is formally reprimanded in writing, demeaned in front of other employees, or scolded for something they did not have the authority, autonomy, or freedom to do or not do. This happens quite

47

often in smaller organizations where the person in charge is the "CEO" and works closely and sometimes too closely to the staff. These leaders often impose their natural decision making abilities that come from a wealth of life experiences to judge what someone should have done. They never took the time to even train them or explicitly give them the authority and autonomy to do whatever it takes to be successful in their role. Every choice or action if not successful was held to the highest levels of consequences. These types of interactions with employees are the breeding ground for toxicity simply because the employee is held accountable for their lack of action with no true authority, autonomy, or freedom to act without repercussions. Can this be altered, absolutely but the person in leadership has to ask themselves:

Can an employee's resourcefulness that leads to a failed outcome result in a negative reprimand for the employee?

If your answer is yes, then keep reading. If it is no, Then what will you do to prevent a future failed outcome in the same scenario? I am never asking a leader not to address a concern. What I am asking of the Leader, is that they LEAD!

"You can never have an impact on society if you have not changed yourself."
– Nelson Mandela

As previously mentioned some of the causes of attrition was based on the role, salary, skillset, and seniority of the employee. It can include the loss of productivity, morale, knowledge, and the expense of recruiting, onboarding, and training a replacement. Take a moment and analyze if there is anything you can do to decrease attrition?

Step One: Cite

"Take nothing on its looks; take everything on evidence. There's no better rule."

-Charles Dickens Great Expectations

Great Expectations by Charles Dickens tells the story of Pip, an English orphan who rises to wealth, deserts his true friends, and becomes humbled by his own arrogance. Utilizing this quote by Charle Dickens is intentional because yes taking things on evidence is true but there is an importance that must be noted. In assessing anything the questions you ask yourself about a given subject or person will drive what "Evidence" you use to make a decision.

The Perception of A Problem

There are times in management when we make statements that describe the cause or causes of an outcome. These statements in some instances can be detrimental to the work culture and a successful intended outcome. Statements like "Nobody is working", "This is your fault", "It's not my responsibility" "The team has high absenteeism"and so forth. All of these phrases when stated without evidence leave them open to interpretation by those they are directed to and all those who hear it. Each person is left in control of how they will assess the statement that was made directly to them, the team, or another in a negative or positive manner. Take for instance "The team has high absenteeism". A person who has never been absent is accused of being absent. What does that do to their trust in leadership? What does that do to their morale when they know they have never missed a day of work? While the absence rate is high there is no evidence to justify addressing this matter as a team when it is a specific individual or individuals.

Effective leaders understand the necessity to address certain issues directly and not in the whole group. If the attendance rate is being impacted by one or two individuals address them directly but not just in word of mouth but with evidence. That evidence then should be followed by questions to the individual to address what you have presented as a leader.

In the person vs the process we "Cite" first.

Cite - evidence for or justification of an argument or statement.

In order to begin to assess whether it is the Person vs the Process one must Cite the problem with evidence. There are a series of questions to ask yourself in this stage:

Question #1: What do you perceive the problem to be?

Perception is everything and what you perceive the problem to be can actually not be the problem at all. In citing you want to provide evidence. The evidence should align to the actions taken in alignment with The Process for the intended outcome. For example, let's take something simple like crossing the street.

Antiquated Analysis:

> **Intended outcome:** Cross the street.
>
> **Outcome:** Did not cross the street.
>
> **Evidence:** No one is across the street.
>
> **Results**: Replace or reprimand the person told to cross the street.

I have coached executives in shifting their mindset from utilizing the Antiquated Analysis Method because it has cost them quality personnel, clients, and in some instances their company. In utilizing this method many executives begin these conversations with the problem and end at the evidence being all they know, or want to know which is all that matters to them. This is a skewed method of management because decisions are made without asking the important questions. The questions we ask are integral to achieving the results we want to accomplish. In addition, as humans we grapple with the subjective versus the objective.

"Most misunderstandings in the world could be avoided if people would simply take the time to ask, "What else could this mean?"
- Shannon L. Alder

The following is what an evolved analysis looks like:

Evolved Analysis:

    Intended Outcome: Crossing the street

    Outcome: Did not cross the street.

    Evidence: No one is across the street.

    Causes: Gap in the road, bolder, speeding cars, the person doesn't know how to cross, The person was never told what road to cross, emotions, etc.

    Results: Implement solutions to the causes and repeat the initially intended outcome.

You may ask yourself what happens if the outcome is the same? This is why we must look at THE PROCESS.

"The Process is only as effective as the knowledge and implementation of the steps necessary to reach the intended outcome consistently"
- Bidoism

The Process

How does a person go from start to finish in order for it to be deemed a successful outcome? This question is probably the most unanswered question in most work environments. The Process of the work is rarely defined to the specificity necessary to hold someone truly accountable. The finish line is skewed and what results in true success is misunderstood and rarely attained by the employee or understood by leadership. The illusion of success is a dangerous workplace habit to have as a norm. The Process needs to be defined by both leadership and employees in order to assess where there is alignment and where the gaps exist.

The Illusion of Success: Wepaaaaaaaa!

Circa 2006 I worked for one of the livest work environments in banking… the Spanish Unit! It was a movie everyday at work as we sat in our fortress of cubicles. Each cubicle had its own decor, some represented their heritage and others a host of family pictures with positive sayings. Our headsets and swivel chairs added to the decor and the maracas and noise makers added to the signature call when you received a payment on someone's late payments. "WEEEEEEEEEEPAAAAAAAAAAAAAAA!"

was accompanied by cheers and clapping from all the representatives not on a call. The entire department was sectioned off by levels of delinquency. From the first level to the last level "Wepaaaaaaa! Didn't change as it was the announcement of what deemed success. New hires began in Level One the least amount of delinquency and the sounds of success were frequent. Payment after payment you would hear short wepas, loud ones, and long ones weeeeeeeeeeeeeeeeeeeeeeeeeeeepa! Imagine every 10 calls a party unfolding. At least that's how it felt and it felt good. I moved on to level two implementing the same process. I wasn't trained in level two or level three. What I started to observe though was as you progressed up the levels of delinquency the "Wepaaaaaa's" were few and far between. Those representatives not meeting the quota would be brought into a group meeting to discuss the data and usually there was pressure placed on representatives by saying their job was on the line or comparing their data to that of a group of representatives responsible for level one delinquency. This wasn't motivating. Even how the level 4 stage through Charge Off yelled wepa was different. It lacked enthusiasm, it was defeated. As I grew tired of the meetings with little to no training, degrading speeches, and threats of unemployment I sought a new job that was more in alignment with the type of work culture I wanted to be in.

I was disappointed in the illusion of success. A year or two later I was contacted by some of the employees about a situation that was occurring. Due to the outcomes being misaligned and the necessity for training in order to meet the numbers some of those who had stayed after I left began doing anything to hit the number. This resulted in the department being under investigation. I won't go into too many details here but it caused the integrity and demise of several people and their career. The tactics they used to succeed cost them everything. Are you asking your employees to do anything to succeed? Are you laying out the clear path to success?

The Impacts of Strategic Planning on the Process

If there was an essential term to know and implement in leadership it would be Strategic Planning. This is imperative in the person vs the process methodology because strategic planning is the art of creating specific business strategies, implementing them, and evaluating the results of executing the plan, in regard to a company's overall long-term goals or desires. Strategic planning became popular in the 1950's and its use declined until around 1990 where it was seen as relevant to modern business. Usually the strategic planning process focuses on Upper-level management and that is okay. What I have found is that there is a step that should occur with staff before upper-level management begins strategizing. That is that all upper management should speak directly to the employees about the process of the work they have been hired to do. Upper management is often so far removed that the goals being set in strategic plans aren't even attainable with the way the work is conducted in frontline roles.

The development and execution of strategic planning are typically viewed as consisting of being performed in three critical steps:

1. Strategy Formulation

In the process of formulating a strategy, a company will first assess its current situation by performing an internal and external audit. The purpose of this is to help identify the organization's strengths and weaknesses, as well as opportunities and threats (SWOT Analysis).

SWOT Analysis

Strengths:

- Identify skills and capabilities that you have.
- What can you do particularly well, relative to rivals?
- What do analysts consider to be your strengths?
- What resources do you have?
- Is your brand or reputation strong?

Weaknesses:

- What do rivals do better than you?
- What do you do poorly?
- What generates the most customer dissatisfaction and complaints?
- What generates the most employee dissatisfaction and complaints?
- What processes and activities can you improve?

Opportunities:

- Where can you apply your strengths?
- How are your customers and their needs changing?
- How is technology changing your business?
- Are there new markets for your strengths? (e.g. foreign)

- Are there new ways of producing your products?
- Are your rivals' customers dissatisfied?

Threats:

- Are customers able to meet their needs with alternative products?
- Are customers' needs changing away from your product?
- What are your competitors developing?
- Are your rivals improving their product offerings or prices?
- Is new technology making your product obsolete?
- Is your cash-flow and debt position healthy?
- Are your employees satisfied? Is turnover high?
- Is new competition coming?
- Are sales growing slower than the industry average?

More than just answering the questions, the most important of concluding questions is what do you do with the information. This is where strategic planning comes to life via implementation.

2. Strategy Implementation

After a strategy is formulated, the company needs to establish specific targets or goals related to putting the strategy into action, and allocate resources for the strategy's execution. The success of the implementation stage is often determined by how good a job upper management does in regard to clearly communicating the chosen strategy throughout the company and getting all of its employees to "buy into" the desire to put the strategy into action. The buy-in is cultivated by the inclusion of the work from the employee lens.

3. Strategy Evaluation

Any savvy business person knows that success today does not guarantee success tomorrow. As such, it is important for managers to evaluate the performance of a chosen strategy after the implementation phase.

Strategy evaluation involves three crucial activities:

- reviewing the internal and external factors affecting the implementation of the strategy
- measuring performance
- taking corrective steps to make the strategy more effective

All three steps in strategic planning occur within three hierarchical levels: upper management, middle management, and operational levels. It is best to start at the operational level because in most cases it offers the most accurate insight of the work. Thus, it is imperative to foster communication and interaction among employees and managers at all levels, to help them operate as a more functional and effective team. While planning requires a significant amount of time, effort, and money, a well-thought-out strategic plan efficiently fosters company growth, goal achievement, and employee satisfaction.

One of the most important factors of the strategic plan is the frequency in which it is referenced during meetings on every level. Often the strategic plan is written and never gone to again until it is time to be updated. The intentionality in which we integrate the strategic plan in our conversations weekly is what keeps our collective focus on the end result. In addition the metrics we include that identify the milestones necessary to ensure success are mapped by the integration of the right data.

The Data That Matters

When it comes to achieving what is outlined within a strategic plan we must look at the milestones on the operational level that drive the outcome. Within a given position there can be several steps and necessary milestones to reach what we call the finish line of the position's responsibility.

Example:

Customer Service Process:

- Make Calls
- Provide customer information for a possible resolution or direct next steps.
- Take Calls
- Provide customer information for a possible resolution or direct next steps.
- Track the results of the Call

If on your strategic plan there is a focus for increasing customer satisfaction out of this process what is a milestone? and What is the finish line? In the previous examples the following are milestones:

- Make Calls
- Take Calls

The finish line is:

- Track the results of the Call

The milestones of a process are those things that drive you to the finish line. Within the goals there should be an expected outcome that takes into consideration success at its minimum time and maximum timeframe. Then the finish line is the actual expected percentage of success. This outcome is concrete: yes you achieved it or no. This is the answer for each call.

This is how the process is cited. Step by step from each position. As a leader I would sit with the employee or the person deemed the expert in that role to glean the exact steps of their position. In addition, I would consistently cite areas where authority for decision making was necessary as that would increase the number of milestones that existed prior to getting to the finish Line.

For example:

Customer Service Process:

- Make Calls
- Get approval for the possible resolution provided.
- Provide customer information for a possible resolution or direct next steps.
- Take Calls
- Get approval for the possible resolution provided.
- Provide customer information for a possible resolution or direct next steps.
- Track the results of the Call

What does this look like for data output:

- Make Calls : Number of calls per day or per hour or both at max and minimum ex. 10 calls per hour = 80 calls per day at 10 min per call. Max.
- Track the results of the Call: Resolution provided yes or no 80 calls 30% resolution yes. 70% resolution no.

This kind of breakdown is how delineated the data needs to be in order to drive next steps effectively. This allows for the questions to be asked about whether the outcome meets expectations or doesn't. What questions would you ask yourself as a leader about these results? Is it the person or the process?

As you go through each goal within your strategic plan and process ask yourself:

What data is priority? and in What format will this data need to be reported, seen, and analyzed?

Visualize all of the relevant information items you would like to have. These important data sets will continue to reveal themselves as you cite the process. Once you have these points, prioritize them to ensure you are clear of your finish line data. Milestones are actions steps to the end goal. Make sure that it is clear to the employee so they don't misconstrue milestones as the end of the work.

Citing The Process

In order to cite you must assess The Process review must be conducted by both the employee and the leader.

Once the steps are defined it allows for the information to be understood for functionality, logic, etc. There are a series of questions that are necessary to understand about how the process transcends to an Evolved Analysis Mindset. In the shift to this mindset the questions matter and the answers to the questions transcend you to the next step in the methodology **Understand**.

CHAPTER TWO: UNDERSTAND

"All truths are easy to understand once they are discovered; the point is to discover them."

-Galileo Galilei

What's Really Going On Here?

Have you ever been at work and asked yourself as a leader "What's really going on here?" The answer to this question could be easy to find in some work environments and in others like walking through a labyrinth at night with a blindfold on. Picture that for a second. Walking through a labyrinth at night with a blindfold on. How fast and far do you think you will get? Throughout my experiences I have observed the separation of departments and responsibilities being so siloed that it impacts outcome on every level of leadership your ability to implement the person vs the process taking place. Silos are perpetuated by a lack of trust, a scarcity mentality, and lack of direction.

"None of us is as smart as all of us."
– Ken Blanchard, Author

Silo Thinking In Leadership

Merriam-Webster Defines A Silo as "an isolated grouping, department, etc., that functions apart from others especially in a way seen as hindering communication and cooperation". There are types of Silo Mentality:

Hierarchical Silo

A top-heavy corporate structure, typically found in big, multinational corporations, would fit this silo mentality definition. Often, you'll see a clear divide between the upper and lower levels of workers. Juniors feel alienated, as important information is rarely shared with them. This leads to red-tapism, employee discontent and high attrition rate.

Divisional Silo

This is caused by a lack of communication between departments, especially when a particular division is only interested in getting its own tasks done. Such attitudes are often fostered by team leaders but can be perpetuated by all employees.

Geographical Silo

A key component is a silo mentality definition, geography plays a significant role in silo situations. Geographical silos can occur when employees of a large organization are located in different cities, countries, or continents. The remote work and time differences hinder regular communication, causing colleagues to work in increasing isolation from one another.

To the list I want to add another that often exists among employees which is:

Individual Silo

A key component of this mentality is that it is seen between individual employees, who may hoard information for their benefit. They see the sharing of information as a direct impact to their employability.

Have you ever experienced any of these types of silo's? How has it impacted your ability to lead? How has silo's impacted how you see the process? What do you believe are some of the effects of "Silo Mentality"?

The Effects of Silo Mentality

Duplicated Work

One might assume that because their roles are different that the duplication of work would be minimized. Unfortunately, this is not the case. Duplicated work is a result of poor communication, unclear organization or in most cases a lack of role clarity. In a report to assess productivity it was noted that many US employees spend almost 6 hours per week doing duplicate work. Out of those employees 51% duplicated work due to a lack of information. These work silos perpetuate this duplication. Those who need to know don't know when something is complete. This is why defining the process is so important. When you know the work you know how and when to integrate proper systems of information delivery that minimize this duplication.

Friction over Responsibilities

When the work isn't clearly defined it is even more difficult to see where there is overlap and friction over responsibilities. Some people with silo mentalities will either say the work is their responsibility or on the other spectrum that it's not their responsibility. The friction levels rise when the lack of definition over responsibilities leads to a negative outcome. This is where the silos become contentious and the blame game begins leading to more time wasted.

Misinformation

Silo mentality is a catalyst to misinformation. It is often the breeding place of assumptions of the work, what has been completed, and a host of things that could be resolved if people just asked. How does one confirm information throughout "The Process"? One must assess if there are hard stops or milestones where confirmation of progress occurs. In the age of all things technology this is where the integration of CRMs and other productivity software can clarify misinformation through the lifecycle of the work.

Decreased overall goal attainment

When people exhibit silos there is a natural decrease in the overall goal attainment by the whole group. There is a saying that says " You are only as strong as your weakest link" and if we are talking about an anchor absolutely but we are speaking about a human being. Human beings can be taught, can evolve, and can transcend. If this wasn't the case people of color would have never transcended the inaccurate imagery of weakness depicted in history books for hundreds of years. The reference of weakness in any scenario should inspire a leader to want to lead and reinforce with professional development, training and resources.

Overall Broken Trust...

But what is TRUST?

The Building Blocks of Trust

One of the best videos I have seen on this topic was a presentation I watched on Building trust | by James Davis | TEDxUSU. In his talk he said the essence of all relationships is trust. It has been said that trust is the glue that holds people, organizations and societies together. Without trust, relationships become rigid, less efficient and economies are slowed. Yet, despite all the studies and platitudes, trust may be one of the most misunderstood, misinterpreted and misapplied aspects of human and organizational relationships.

He defined Trust as:

Choosing to be vulnerable and take risks.

He further elaborated that we must have the propensity to trust also known as the ability to take on that vulnerability. He identified three drivers of trust:

Ability

Can that person do what they say they do?

He emphasized that ability is situation specific. It is specific to the thing they say they will do.

Benevolence

Do they care about me?

If they care about me it is not driven by their ego. They don't care about me for their own gratification.

Integrity

Having a set of values that you live by and other people agree with those values?

It is perceived integrity as they trust you to be everything you say you will do or be.

In any leadership style people have to trust you and your ability to lead. This takes the willingness to understand what it takes for someone to trust you.

Alignment of Trust

As referenced previously in the "Building Trust" there are 3 things that needed to be present which were ability, benevolence, and integrity. Where do these align in The Person vs The Process. It aligns across the board. For instance,

The Person has to have the Ability

The Person has to have Benevolence

The Person has to have Integrity

And

The Process has to provide the Ability to work.

The Process has to provide the Benevolence not to cause harm.

The Process has to provide the integrity to be consistent to its intended outcome.

They both have to align to ensure the outcome.If you have a person with the ability but the process does not provide the ability for a successful outcome there will be a conflict. If you have a person of benevolence with a process that produces the opposite of benevolence it will cause a conflict. If you have a person with integrity and the process in the opposite, then you will have conflicts. Through all of these conflicts the role of the leader is to understand what needs to be addressed. This is the reason we start with Understanding the Process and then The Person.

These drivers of trust are built by the authentic intentional practice of understanding the work as a leader. When was the last time you felt understood in your work environment? When was the last time you understood the work you were called to do specifically?

The Importance of Understanding

Have you taken the time to understand your work or the work of others you are responsible for ensuring their success? All the answers to the previous questions matter when implementing the person vs the process.

Step Two: Understand

Understand-interpret or view (something) in a particular way.

To understand something is to take the time to interpret and view it in a particular way. By taking the time to understand the intended outcome, the outcome, the evidence, and the causes enable you as a leader the power to grasp what is occurring in the given scenario. More importantly it is in the understanding of the work that allows for true improvements and leadership to rise to any occasion for driving success.

Understanding The Process

I teach the necessity for understanding so we as leaders don't continue the cycle of blame. When I ask what do you understand about the process it forces a pause even in the most experienced person. If you don't understand how the work is done then how do you implement corrective measures? How do you direct success? And How do you hold people accountable ethically?

Don Sherman wrote an article in Car and Magazine titled: "How a Car is Made: Every Step from Invention to Launch "We layed out **the process** of vehicle creation from start to finish."

In this article he stated:

- It was the first time we've presented the entire start-to-finish plan
- Separated into five categories.
- The end is when the new model reaches showrooms.
- On average, the entire process takes 72 months.
- There's overlap to save time, as revealed by the start and finish months listed in each of the five category headings.

Let's take a moment to acknowledge the first statement he made "It was the <u>first time</u> we've presented the entire start-to-finish plan". In 1885, German mechanical engineer Karl Benz designed and built the world's first practical automobile to be powered by an internal-combustion engine. On January 29, 1886, Benz received the first patent (DRP No. 37435) for a gas-fueled car. It was a three-wheeler; Benz built his first four-wheeled car in 1891. Benz & Cie., the company started by the inventor, became the world's largest manufacturer of automobiles by 1900. Benz was the first inventor to integrate an internal combustion engine with a chassis - designing both together. Don Sherman published his article November 18, 2015 in Car & Driver Magazine. That to me is a pretty long time for it to be the first time it was done. Its existence in writing are the foundations and the makings of future manufacturers.

Don Sherman synthesized the list of categories and sub-tasks identified by two manufacturing companies the following is only one of the categories:

I. INVENTION:MONTHS 0–72

1. Research market, including in-house and field investigations, to identify the role of this product and its components in the global

portfolio; define separation from similar models sold by sister brands

2. Identify special features, advantages, and potential world, U.S., or segment firsts

3. Define competitive set, target customers; set curb-weight, fuel-economy, and performance goals

4. Competitive assessment

5. Powertrain selection

6. Budget, funding, pricing, investment considerations

7. Computer-aided-engineering (CAE) analysis

8. Customer, press, analyst clinics

His steps are an example of understanding the process yet as it relates to the internal workings of the company or organization this is the version I implore leaders to understand:

Example:

Car Manufacturing Process as outlined by Don Sherman

Step 1. INVENTION   **Duration:**

MONTHS 0–72

1. Research market, including in-house and field investigations, to identify the role of this product and its components in the global portfolio; define separation from similar models sold by sister brands

2. Identify special features, advantages, and potential world, U.S., or segment firsts

3. Define competitive set, target customers; set curb-weight, fuel-economy, and performance goals

4. Competitive assessment

5. Powertrain selection

6. Budget, funding, pricing, investment considerations
7. Computer-aided-engineering (CAE) analysis
8. Customer, press, analyst clinics

The Person vs The Process Methodology: Car Manufacturing Process

Step 1. INVENTION   **Duration: TBD**

1. Research market including in-house and field investigations to identify the role of this product and its components in the global portfolio.
2. Define separation from similar models sold by sister brands
3. Identify special features
4. Identify advantages
5. Identify potential world U.S., or segment firsts
6. Define competitive set,
7. Define target customers
8. Define set curb-weight
9. Define fuel-economy
10. Define performance goals
11. Competitive assessment
12. Powertrain selection
13. Budget
14. Funding
15. Pricing
16. Investment considerations
17. Computer-aided-engineering (CAE) analysis
18. Customer
19. Press
20. Analyst clinics

Why do I have 20 steps versus the original identified 8? Because each of those steps have independent processes no matter the number of people who carry out the steps. Implementing the separation is where I find efficiency gaps, overlap of work, inaccurate ratios between staffing numbers to the workload, unrealistic goal setting and employee outcomes, and a host of other information that helps guide not only Leadership's understanding of the work but the employees understanding of their role as well.

To understand takes you as a leader to want to dive deeper to understand. In The Person vs The Process this is integral to analyzing next steps for sustainable success in any work environment and the culture that breeds success. The following steps assist you in being able to understand any situation from an objective versus subjective perspective when you put yourself in the place of the person under review:

1. What would you do in the scenario?
2. What resources do you have to support the success of your answer?
3. What previous experience and or knowledge do you have that allows you to implement your prospective solution?
4. Does the employee have similar experiences and knowledge?
5. Have you trained this employee?
6. Has anyone trained this employee?

After answering the previous question What does it reveal about the person? What does it reveal about the process? What does this reveal about your role as a leader?

After you answer these questions it is time to **REFLECT.**

CHAPTER THREE: REFLECT

"Reflection is one of the most underused yet powerful tools for success."

-Richard Carlson

The Style of Leadership

When it comes to The Person vs The Process it is important to understand your Leadership style or styles. Leadership Style is defined as the classification of how a person behaves while directing, motivating, guiding, and managing groups of people. Leadership styles can be chosen or imposed on an individual person as a result of their work environment. Leadership Style can have a direct impact on The Person and The Process. There is a leadership style that uses this methodology effectively.

Types of Leadership Styles

The following are the identified list of Leadership Styles. Have you identified which leadership styles align with a leader? Some companies ask this question of their leaders in personality tests and other forms of questioning. What would employees say your leadership style is? Is it the same as the one you selected? Has the question ever been asked of employees?

Do you think you are a Servant Leader while your employees think you are Bureaucratic? In reflecting on the work leadership is integral to what happens next in employee outcomes. Identify your leadership style and reflect on what evidence exists that you exhibit these characteristics? Is it the best fit for your work environment?

Transformational Leadership

is a leadership style that empowers people to accomplish positive change through big vision, inspiration, and a call to action. Leaders enable change by emotionally connecting with their audience and inspiring them to achieve something greater than themselves.

Transactional Leadership

is a managerial style that relies on attaining goals through structure, supervision and a system of rewards and punishments. This results-oriented approach works well with self-motivated employees. It doesn't focus on changing or improving the organization as a whole, but instead, aims to hit short-term goals while establishing unity and conformity with the company. The rewards or punishments are, therefore, referred to as the "transaction."

Servant Leadership

is a management style in which you focus on your team's growth and well-being to put their needs first. The theory is that instead of employees serving the leader, the leader serves the employees. This type of manager believes that when their team members feel personally and professionally fulfilled, they produce high-quality work more efficiently and productively. Employee satisfaction and collaboration are important concepts in servant leadership. You can use this leadership style in any type of business but it is particularly popular within nonprofit organizations.

Strategic Leadership

happens when a leader shares a vision and goal with their team and inspires them to work together to reach it. A strategic leader often acts as the motivating force for an organization, letting individuals know their role in achieving the vision. This leadership style helps others have direction at all times.

Autocratic Leadership

also known as authoritarian leadership, is a leadership style characterized by individual control over all decisions and little input from group members.typically make choices based on their ideas and judgments and rarely accept advice from followers. Autocratic leadership involves absolute, authoritarian control over a group.

Democratic Leadership

also known as participative leadership or shared leadership, is a leadership style in which members of the group participate in the decision-making process. This type of leadership can apply to any organization, from private businesses to schools to the government.Everyone is given the opportunity to participate, ideas are exchanged freely, and discussion is encouraged. While this process tends to focus on group equality and the free flow of ideas, the democratic leader is still there to offer guidance and control.

Laissez-faire Leadership

also known as delegative leadership, is a type of leadership style in which leaders are hands-off and allow group members to make the decisions. Researchers have found that this is generally the leadership style that leads to the lowest productivity among group members.

Situational Leadership

is a leadership style in which a leader adapts their style of leading to suit the current work environment and/or needs of a team.

Bureaucratic Leadership

is a leadership style that follows a hierarchy where formal duties are fixed. Leaders using this approach function per official rules set by superiors within the company. Employees under this leadership follow specific authority and regulations developed by their managers.

Charismatic Leadership

is defined by a leader who uses his or her communication skills, persuasiveness, and charm to influence others. Charismatic leaders, given their ability to connect with people on a deep level, are especially valuable within organizations that are facing a crisis or are struggling to move forward.

Coaching Leadership

is a leadership style that requires you to focus on the needs of your team. It involves identifying the strengths and weaknesses of your overall team and of individual members. By knowing how to become a coaching leader, you can help empower your team and create more clear communication in the workplace.

Visionary Leadership

is a leadership style that is futuristic, innovative and imaginative. Visionary leaders have the ability to see the big picture, and imagine new ways to paint that picture. They have a compelling vision of the future, where they can make a positive impact and, often, disrupt the status quo.

Participative Leadership

is a style of leadership in which all members of the organization work together to make decisions. Participative leadership is also known as democratic leadership, as management teams encourage all employees to participate.

Adaptive Leadership

A practical leadership framework that helps individuals and organizations adapt and thrive in challenging environments.

Work Imposed Leadership Style (WILS)

There are work environments that condition your leadership style. There are leadership styles that are a catalyst for successful outcomes. While others can be so detrimental to the work environment that it is the very reason it fails to attain the intended outcome. WILS can create a behavior in you that is not in alignment with the type of person you are. Take for instance a work environment that sees little value in the input from anyone can be deemed as an Autocratic Leadership Style. Though Autocratic at work you may be the type of person who doesn't believe in an Autocratic Leadership Style thus overtime this will either filter into other settings outside of work and or take a complete toll on you as a person. The pressures of having to live up to an Autocratic Leadership Style can subsequently impact your mental health. In addition, this can also impact the mental health of those who fall under your leadership impact as a result of zero feedback or room for advice. Any setting that doesn't have a space for feedback or input from employees as it relates to the work has a direct impact on The Process. In a WILS environment the individual task with leadership will have to make the ultimate decision as to whether or not the work environment is a fit.

Self Imposed Leadership Style (SILS)

Self Imposed Leadership Styles are chosen by the individual leader. The work environment is fluid and the governance allows for those tasked with leadership to lead how they see fit essentially. In these settings your personal experience being in a leadership position coupled with your roles and responsibilities can have you self impose a leadership style that may or may not be a fit for you or your work environment. For instance, if you are a leader with years of work experience leading and mentoring employees when a problem arises your self imposed leadership style will be able to navigate the situation accordingly with little to no fall out. If you are a novice at leading when a situation arises you may find yourself shifting through different leadership styles. This shift can be successful or it can lead to a misunderstanding between you and your staff. This then creates a culture where your staff exhibits feelings of lack of trust, disdain, frustration, and a list of other behaviors that cause them to lose respect for you.

The Servant Leader

In the book authored by Joel Bialy "The Servant Leader" he summarizes the Four Dimensions of Leadership:

- The head (assumptions and thinking)
- The hands (application and leadership behavior)
- The heart (motives and EGO—Edging God Out or Exalting God Only)
- The habits (solitude, prayer, study of scripture, unconditional love, etc.)

Within this delineation the following 12 characteristic were highlighted:

1. Servant leaders start by listening
2. Servant leaders are empathetic
3. Servant leaders strive to "know the unknowable"
4. Servant leaders have foresight
5. Servant leaders serve without limits
6. Servant leaders are people-builders rather than people-users
7. Servant leaders are humble
8. Servant leaders have integrity
9. Servant leaders know what they're in service of

10. Service organizations are themselves servants

11. Service leaders are first amongst equals

12. The world needs you to serve

Of all the leadership styles I emphasize the Servant Leader because this is the style it takes to want to even implement this type of methodology.

Step Three: Reflect

Reflect - think deeply or carefully about.

To reflect is to think deeply or carefully by definition. One might believe that thinking deeply or carefully takes days or weeks. To think deeply and carefully isn't about time, it is about focus. In work environments I have observed people arrive at work at 7 am in the morning and from 3 to 5 produce more work than they did the entire day. Was this about time or was this about Focus. With this in mind in this stage it is necessary to reflect on the following:

1. What is the intended outcome?

2. What is the process?

3. What does the person responsible for this need to know how to do?

4. Based on the process, what adjustments need to be made to support the intended outcome?

5. What is the process for the person responsible to make changes to the process?

The answers to these questions will give you the foundational information needed to **EMPOWER**.

CHAPTER FOUR: EMPOWER

"My faith plus my hustle will alway make me a winner"

-Bidoism

Faith Above All

In the essence of authenticity there is no way I can speak of empowerment without solidifying the fact that my ability to lead was rooted in FAITH. The ability to empower others in anything is because I was being empowered through the God within me coupled with a relentless spirit to succeed. Success not for self but for the affirmation of God's gifts and their use to empower others to believe in themselves and above all my relentless Faith in God. I remember the days when challenges arose in my work environment and the verses situated all around my cubicle reminded me of the strength within me, the words affirming that God would never leave me, that no weapon formed against me would prosper, that my foot would be set upon a rock, that everything is for my good, and the list goes on. This is not to convert you but to confirm without a shadow of a doubt where the audacity to even write this book comes from. May you utilize your faith within your leadership practice to empower others because I certainly know I did.

What Is Empowerment?

Empowerment is defined as the "process that fosters power in people for use in their own lives, their communities, and their society, by acting on issues they define as important" (Page & Czuba, 1999). Empowerment allows you to feel confident that you possess the power necessary to create the life you want and develop the belief that you are capable of accomplishing anything you set your mind to. Muhammad Ali was a perfect example of this belief as one of my favorite quotes that graced my desk and vision board was:

I am gonna show you how GREAT I AM.
-Muhammad Ali

This is the essence of faith coupled with action. To show your greatness in everything you do. To model greatness as a leader for others to know it is possible. Within the person vs the process it is integral that Leaders are able to empower others to see themselves as great and support them to actually be great in the work they have been tasked to do.

The benefits of feeling empowered is that it allows for the pursuit of goals no matter what the goals are. When you believe you can, your actions will drive you to achievement. One study used an online psycho-educational program to help treat people with depression and measured changes in empowerment. Immediately following the program, participants noted an increase in self-esteem and empowerment. Improvements in their quality of life were noted even six months after the completion of the program (Crisp et al., 2014). This means that improving your self-esteem and feeling more empowered can have a positive effect on your overall quality of life.

Examples of Empowerment

What are the examples of empowerment around you? Does it start with the person in the mirror? As a leader we have to believe in our own abilities in order to pour into others. I had examples of empowerment all around me in and out of my work environment. But when they existed in my work environment it solidified the existence of more. My vision was amplified because my mentors became lanterns shining a light on the path to success and the array of opportunities that existed as an Educated Latina. What couldn't I aspire to do or be. I remember vividly when I was a Truancy Officer for Newark Public Schools and I had the honor of being in a room 5 days a week with Three Alpha Men who poured into me a standard of excellence and audacity that propelled me to the next level not just in my career but in life. That year with Dr. Stephen Webb, Musa Abdullah, and Pastor Damon Gilyard changed the very essence of my womanhood as they indoctrinated me in the power within me. They would sit me down to watch documentaries on shifting my mindset. Musa Abdullah, a man of Alphi Phi Alpha Fraternity whose height alone would put me on notice would look me up and down and immediately pose a question that would set the tone for intellectual sparring that would have me assessing everything I thought I knew about everything and anything. He handed me this book called 'The Science of Getting Rich" by Wallace D. Wattles and Musa said "be careful that's a heavy lift now, I don't know if you are ready for that." to which I would answer "I am ready".

It was my belief in myself and their belief in me that is the catalyst to completing my degree. Dr. Webb said "Time will pass and either you will be one class closer to your Doctorate or not, either way time passes". What I learned was priceless and I showed them my gratitude by living up to everything they saw in me then. When I was no longer in their presence I had to continue empowering myself.

Empowering Yourself

Within leadership you have to develop self-empowerment. The challenges that arise in leadership will test you to the very core. Especially, when you are responsible for the outcomes of other individuals. I had to develop a set of go-to tactics to survive the calling of leadership and empowerment of others. It began with utilizing positive self-talk. Utilizing the correct words held a profound power in my ability to focus on the solution to a matter. It allowed for others to be empowered around me because the words I would use were to direct positive action steps. For example, instead of thinking "I can't do that", I think "I love challenging things". This simple switch has made a world of difference for me. I utilized positive self-affirmation to drive my thoughts as well. I am brilliant, I am indomitable, I am resilient, I am noble, and so forth. Not only would I say them to myself I would have them posted on sticky notes or on a vision board.

I created a list of career goals I set for myself within my position. What was deemed success in my career? By defining these things it provided a reference point for the actions I should be doing on a daily basis. Empowered people recognize the need to put in the work to reach their goals.

I know without a shadow of a doubt I had to be sound if what I knew that I knew. When I walked into rooms with individuals that may have had longer tenure, experience, or a title I was confident in my expertise. That belief was imperative in navigating the rooms where I was one of one in gender and race. As Robin Sharma said, "Speak your truth even if your voice shakes." But my voice wasn't shaking, "I was refined by the fire and came out as pure gold."

Empowerment Theory

Empowerment theory is a framework to help motivate people to take charge of their own life. It has been used in various settings to assist people from all walks of life in taking back power over what happens to them. Empowerment theory encourages "purposefully participating in a process of changing oneself and one's environment, recognizing patterns, and engaging inner resources for well-being." (Crawford Shearer & Reed, 2016).

Empowerment theory gives people the tools to recognize their ability to participate in their own life. This framework encourages people to use their personal and social resources to play an active, rather than passive, role in working toward their goals.

Empowering vs Enabling

Empowering others can be beneficial for everyone involved but it is important to recognize when it has slipped into enabling behavior. Enabling occurs when you try to help someone but end up supporting their bad behavior or habits. Unfortunately, sometimes kindness can be taken advantage of which is why it is important to be aware of the help you are giving someone and how it is being received. Empowerment means you build them up to do the work themselves; enabling means you are doing the work for them. As a leader, it is important to model empowerment and to build it within your employees. Employees who feel empowered at work will likely feel more motivated to work toward the goals of the company because they feel capable and appreciated. It has been found that increased employee empowerment is associated with increased job and customer satisfaction (Ugboro & Obeng, 2000). This empowerment comes in many forms from one-to-one meetings to professional development necessary to be successful in your work environment.

Professional Development

Professional development is improving yourself through learning and training to advance your career and personal growth in some cases. I believe it can exist within all sizes of organization. There is information we can access online that if packaged can be the foundation of professional development for companies and organizations providing opportunities for growth. What is never ever okay, is to have a group of people work for you in any capacity and receive zero opportunities for growth whether personal or professional. I have found that companies with sound professional development practices could easily answer whether it was the person vs the process because how they educated the team on the work was so thoughtful that it only pointed to the person.

When was the last time you were provided professional development as a leader? When was the last time you provided it for others? There is a misconception that professional development has to be this grand spectacle of speakers and consultants but no. If the budget is there those things are great but when the budget is not available how do you look within your organization at the personnel and extract from it the content area experts that exist. I have come across some employees that should have been in leadership because they were able to coach their fellow coworkers in becoming excellent at their position. Some of them created resources that would ultimately change how the company tracked data or managed the overall process of their business. There are other benefits of professional development for instance:

Improves Confidence - Professional development can increase your confidence as an employee.

Enhances hiring potential - Professional development can enhance your hiring potential because you increase your knowledge, skills and competencies.

Develops skills -Through professional development, you may increase both hard and soft skills within the workplace. Hard skills refer to job-specific knowledge you receive through training or education, while soft skills are personal habits that define how you work, such as communication. Developing your skills can help you become an expert in your field, share your knowledge with new employees or discover opportunities for career advancement.

Increases job opportunities -They could see how you're becoming more knowledgeable and skilled but also that you're an independent learner.

Expands networking opportunities - Professional development can also increase your ability to network through events that many professionals attend, such as:

- Seminars
- Webinars
- Conferences
- Workshops
- Volunteer events

- Classes or programs

These events typically welcome professionals from within your industry, making them valuable ways to meet experts and influencers in your field.

Provides mentorship - Another way to improve your professional development is to find a mentor or role model. A mentor can help guide you and ensure that you're meeting your goals.

Everything that is offered to personnel on an operational level should be offered on an administrative level. Too often the mistake is made when we transcend into leadership that the learning ends and it shouldn't. At the leadership level you should be developing new skills or enhancing the ones you have to a level of mastery that makes you a content area expert. This doesn't just help your organization but opens new opportunities for sharing your expertise as an industry leader. I tell leaders all the time that their knowledge should be shared and published in their own voice. Whether via a Youtube, White Paper, Article, Blog, or formal workshop your expertise should be elevated for all to hear.

Training the Trainer to Train

A quick mention on training. There must be intentionality in those we bring to train. Training must move people from one level of expertise to the next. There should be some understanding of where people are before they walk into the room. In teaching one of the best things that they do in some districts is the use of a Learning Scale. This scale allows for the group to align to a specific level of knowledge upon entering the room. For example, when is train people on grant writing my learning scale in its simplest form looks like this:

0 - I don't know what a grant is.

1- I know what a grant is and have never written a grant.

2 - I have worked with a team to provide information for a grant but have never written one.

3 - I have written a grant but am not an expert in grant writing

4 - I have written a grant and need information on writing a grant for a foundation local municipality, or Federal Level

5- I have written and won a grant.

From the start I pose the question, Where are you on this learning scale? The participants write this on a note, chart paper, jam board etc. This provides an immediate understanding of who is in the room and how my training needs to adjust to ensure people can walk away with new knowledge. It also lets me know what other training may be necessary if everyone in the room was on level 4 or 5. When trainers can't adjust to their audience it can cause frustration in the staff because they value their time. As a leader it is important when we are assessing the person vs the process that we understand what training was truly provided. How do you know what they were meant to receive from training they obtained? Leadership should always provide opportunities for the confirmation of learning. Why? The reason this is necessary is because this is what we hold people to when we are evaluating performance. In some instances, leaders are taking the fact that a training was conducted as the confirmation that what was taught was understood. This is not always the case. Many times employees are present for training, actively participate, yet don't understand how it transcends into the work they do. In moments like this the explicit depiction of how it transcends should be modeled and used within the training example.

Learning + Understanding + Application of Understanding = Training Success

The Messenger Matters

In all things leadership the "Messenger Matters". If you want to have people go through training on how to do a specific task or work process it would be important to select a staff member who actually excels at the task. Far too often nepotism in work environments has fueled a toxic culture. I don't have a problem with nepotism when the person can actually do the work. Too often the person is not qualified and because of their relationship with leadership are the catalyst to low morale and attrition. In several cases, these were the people with the most aggressive behaviors of communication, did the least amount of work, and couldn't be asked about the most menial processes because they would immediately say "That's not my job, that's yours". If this is the messenger, then we know why the culture can be impacted. There is also a need for external messengers. External messengers bring a sense of neutrality that is necessary for authentic engagement for specific training topics and needs. While the messenger matters we must keep in mind the many ways in which people learn.

The Acknowledgement of Learning Styles

Learning Styles are an individual's preferred method of processing information. It is how they collect, understand new knowledge, and retain new knowledge. Learning Styles impact how people learn in various environments both personal and professional. Learning Styles are truly important in how you lead people to success in any environment and especially important in assessing The Person vs The Process. As I typed this very sentence I reflected on the fact that as I was coming up in education there wasn't a form that I ever filled out that affirmed for me or informed my parents what type of learning style I had. In addition, I found that the only time I ever really acknowledged my learning style was in my profession when we discussed it in education classes or with other educators as we developed lesson plans. This acknowledgement of learning styles was profound because it is essential in how we teach people. If in professional development within organizations we don't offer training in various mediums we are ensuring that some people will implement the knowledge faster than others and in some cases there are people who won't get the knowledge at all simply because we didn't vary how it was taught.

"It has been said that 80% of what people learn is visual."
- Allen Klein

The 8 Types of Learning Styles

Neil D. Fleming for over 20 years facilitated workshops on a variety of topics as an educator; it led him to want to deepen his understanding of how people learned and understood information as well as in what way they learned. In 1987, Fleming utilized the Barbe's Vak model to develop his theory. At that time, identified learning styles were only three in number and Fleming added a fourth. In order to determine the initial learning styles family known as the VARK model, Fleming designed a learning style questionnaire. There are currently 8 identified Learning styles that exist to help you learn as you engage in training currently or throughout your career. Not understanding your learning style can impede your success. So what Learning Style do you have? The following are the 8 learning Styles:

- Visual Learning Style
- Auditory Learning
- Reading/Writing Learning
- Kinesthetic Learning
- Logical Learning
- Social Learning

- Solitary Learning
- Naturalistic Learning

Over time I realized that my style depended upon the subject matter or the task before me. When I was in bootcamp learning how the 1's and 0's worked in Technology there was nothing about it that I would have understood without the visual and kinesthetic training style of the teacher.

Step Four: Empower

Empower -give (someone) the authority or power to do something. To empower an individual is to give them the tools in conjunction with the mental affirmation needed to achieve the intended outcome. There are an array of situations where work cultures have been impacted by negative management. They have pointed the finger and blamed everyone for not achieving the outcome. Some people pride themselves with this misplaced sense of power. They never acknowledge the tools that were missing, the lack of empowerment, nor the lack of their own understanding of the work. If the intended outcome is valued then the people producing the outcome should be valued as well if not more. To empower supports the point of the methodology which is to identify whether it is the person or the process. Once the personnel has been empowered with the tools and mental affirmation that they can achieve the intended outcome it is time to **IMPLEMENT**.

PART II

"The most authentic thing about us is our capacity to create, to overcome, to endure, to transform, to love and to be greater than our suffering."
— Ben Okri

CHAPTER FIVE : IMPLEMENT

"Execution without vision is just passing time."

– Henry Ford

The Person

Person: a human being regarded as an individual

The reason that the person is assessed in the person vs the process is simply because too often in leadership we make assumptions about the people we lead and the things they are responsible for doing in their position. Too often we don't take the time to understand how pivotal the ability to produce the expected outcome is to achieving the goals we have agreed to meet. The human being is a vessel full of varied experiences and abilities. To lead them blindly is a disservice to the fidelity of leadership. In the spaces where I have had the honor of observing people in roles it was necessary for me to ask them questions about their understanding of what they have been called to do. In all cases there were some concrete things the person understood and the others assumptions. Those assumptions are what led to a lack of achievement in alignment with the goals.

In leadership it is our responsibility to ask these questions so that we can:

A. Assign people to positions that are best suited to their abilities

B. Train people in the areas that they need in order to be successful in their position

C. Understand if there are things within the process that need improvement

In order to be able to reach the people we lead we have to be conscious of our communication styles. I am a firm believer in "Say what you mean and mean what you say" communication. The worst experiences as an employee is when you are being miscommunicated about what needs to be done. Especially if you are then held accountable for a result you were never privy to. Changes happen true but how changes are navigated in communication are integral to building a positive and successful work culture.

Communication Styles

What is your understanding of your own communication style as a leader? Do you know what it is? Do you utilize different styles depending on the situation? All this matters in leadership. Here are the styles of communication:

Passive

Passive communication refers to avoiding saying what one thinks and feels. Passive communication styles include overall patterns of submissive attitudes, people-pleasing tendencies, and deferring to others' preferences. People with this communication style avoid stating their thoughts and opinions to avoid conflict, discomfort, or guilt associated with self-advocating.

Aggressive

Aggressive communication involves communicating in a way that disregards the needs and feelings of others and instead prioritizes their agenda. Aggressive communicators may interrupt others and often have trouble listening to or acknowledging different perspectives.

Passive-Aggressive

People who act passive-aggressively struggle to be assertive with their needs and feelings. They typically want to avoid conflict or maintain some sense of control in a relationship. Instead of sharing what's honestly on their mind, the behavior can range from mild, snarky comments to gaslighting or emotional manipulation.

There is one more type of communication that has to be identified specifically for work environments and that is written communication. As a result of aggressive, passive aggressive, and passive communication it is necessary to highlight the need to understand written tone. I have seen written communication get lost in translation and create conflict because best-practices for written communication were not utilized. Written communication is any written message that two or more people exchange. Written communication is typically more formal but less efficient than oral communication. Examples of written communication include:

- Emails
- Text messages
- Blog posts
- Business letters
- Reports
- Proposals
- Contracts
- Job descriptions
- Employee manuals
- Memos
- Bulletins
- Instant messages
- Postcards
- Faxes
- Advertisements
- Brochures
- News releases
- Most businesses require and depend on written communication to function and share information.

Qualities of effective written communication

All effective forms of written communication have these qualities:

Comprehensive: Includes all the relevant details

Accurate: All details are correct

Appropriate: Has the right tone and level of formality

Composition: Has correct spelling and grammar

Clear: Is understandable

But why speak about communication in the stage of implementation? This is because we must ensure that how we communicate goals and expectations are clear. In addition, it is necessary that we as elite leaders use the proper communication style when implementing corrective actions when necessary. It is at the implementation stage where employees are led to success or fall short of it. This is where we will see the evidence to answer whether it is the person or the process. The implementation of everything we have been trained and called to do will provide direction if we choose to seek it.

Step Five: Implement

Implement -put (a decision, plan, agreement, etc.) into effect. At this stage the process is cited for milestones and understood. Goals have been communicated effectively. At the implementation stage all parties should be clear on the intended outcome, their roles in achieving the intended outcomes, resources are present, and avenues to seek support at points of the process are in place. Once the implementation has occurred it is time to survey the outcome.

CHAPTER SIX: SURVEY

"It is a capital mistake to theorize before one has data."

- Arthur Conan Doyle (writing as Sherlock Holmes)

What do you see?

We have now arrived at the pinnacle of this entire process.

Survey - look carefully and thoroughly at (someone or something)
When you go to survey the outcome of a process and the impact a person has on the outcome there are two types of data that exist. During my dissertation I found that both methods are necessary for assessing a full picture of a given goal or expected outcome and they are Quantitative Data and Qualitative Data. Not independent of each other but used in conjunction with each other to ensure that what we see in the data is accurate. The following example will provide the justification for both:

It was a cold winter morning, and the exam was scheduled to begin promptly at 8 am. 30 people were scheduled to take the exam and they would be split evenly in two rooms. The exam was a series of handwritten essays and multiple choice questions with a time limit of 6 hours. After 6 hours the exam concluded.

The quantitative results of the test were pass or fail:

Pass = 15

Fail = 15

Based on the results, what do we see?

Initially we could say that:

- 50% of those who took the exam passed and 50 % failed.

- 50% of those who took the exam were not capable of passing.

- 50% of those who attended were prepared.

The qualitative results were based on 1:1 post interviews with the participants who failed and the following was noted:

- Interview 1: Participant stated that there wasn't any heat in the classroom they were in. After about two hours into the exams their hands grew numb.

- Interview 2: Participant stated that there wasn't any heat in the classroom. That throughout the exam they would have to stop and put their gloves back on in order to feel their fingertips. This caused a lot of time to pass and they could not complete the essay portion of the exam.

- Interview 3: Participant stated that it was so cold in the classroom they were in that they decided to completely forfeit their exam and walked out. This resulted in an automatic fail because they had already started the exam.

Now after reading the qualitative results how has this shifted your thoughts of the quantitative data? This is why utilizing both forms of data is important in how we survey results within a work environment.

As you continue to assess data outcomes, think about what clean data looks like from quantitative aspects. Data cleaning is the process of removing inherent errors in data that might distort your analysis or render it less valuable. Cleaning can come in different forms, including deleting empty cells or rows, removing outliers, and standardizing inputs. The goal of data cleaning is to ensure there are no errors (or as few as possible) that could influence your final analysis.

There is a necessity in data analysis that post collection that we are identifying the right questions to derive the answers to for what is collected. These questions should be easily measurable and closely related to a specific business problem. If the request for analysis is coming from a business team, ask them to provide explicit details about what they're hoping to learn, what they expect to learn, and how they'll use the information. You can use their input to determine which questions take priority in your analysis as a leader.

It is helpful to break the data down into outputs that answer the question. For instance if its quantitative in nature use charts, trends, etc. to assist in visualizing the impact of a specific data set. Qualitative codifying major themes in the data assists in understanding the deeper issues in a process or company practice. In addition, it is important to show how the data at the operational level impacts the organization as a whole.

Step Six: Survey

Survey - look carefully and thoroughly at (someone or something) There are a series of questions that need to be answered:

1. Was the intended outcome achieved?
2. Ask the person responsible, was there anything in the process that impacted the results negative or positive?
3. Ask the person did they have the resources necessary to achieve the process?
4. Were you adequately trained to perform the task?

Now that we have gone through the CURE IS Method, the most important question anyone in management needs to ask themselves before any decision is made is "How does my role affect the intended outcome?" Sometimes the person in question is you. Do you know the work? Are you empowering others with resources and tools? Or are you just pointing the finger, seeking to blame, and leaving successful outcomes to chance? These questions are imperative to understanding the culture that one's style of management imposes on others and how it affects productivity. The person or the process is not to take away the accountability for a person to produce but empowers them to want to do so. Micromanagement as a way of managing others is a sign of two things "The person you hired isn't qualified in your eyes? Or "You are not an effective trainer?" and when there is a gap in the professional development of personnel there is a gap in the knowledge that exists in regards to the work. Ultimately, this process is to coach you into being a better leader who uses higher level thinking to empower others to achieve the intended outcome.

CHAPTER SEVEN: THE JOURNEY TO LEADERSHIP

"Don't be in a hurry to condemn because he doesn't do what you do or think as you think or as fast. There was a time when you didn't know what you know today."

-Malcolm X

Never Forget The Road You've Traveled

When I was in bootcamp I remember my RDC as we exercised to the point of exhaustion would have us say "Because I wanted this one, because I wanted this two, because I wanted this three". It was a constant reminder that whatever I was going through was my own doing. Upon graduating I entered what we call "The Fleet". Up to that moment all I had known about leadership was excellence in bootcamp and that was no longer. I was stationed in places where being a woman in the military was still not fully accepted by those who earned their rank long before I even thought of joining. Being a woman of color was still something that for some in leadership brought them disdain to their core. Sometimes they could and would use their rank to project that energy onto me. I never knew being a Dominican and Puerto Rican Latina for Newark, New Jersey was such an anomaly to some people that upon meeting me they would say "Are you black and white mix" or "Mexican". One day my fellow shipmate from Oregon asked if she could touch my hair as I would wear it out and curly. To this request I said absolutely not in true Leo form. These moments made me question everything I had learned in boot camp about leadership as I met people who would mentor me throughout my time in the Navy and those whose lack of leadership propelled my want to move up in rank so that I could model what leadership should be like. The Navy taught me that leadership has a lot to do with how you handle your own experiences in life. Did it make you bitter? or Did they make you better?

The better was by intention. There were people throughout all of my career settings that exhibited both. Some modeled everything I wanted to be as a leader and others traumatized me and I had to work hard not to become just like them. I had to make decisions about my career that led to me leaving certain places because my mental health and patience were being tested in ways that the reward via opportunity and money were not worth it. I had changed my setting to evolve to the leader I am today. I had to help make a way for others to be able to lead as well so that what was done for me was not in vain. I remember not knowing everything yet those who saw something in me would pull me to the side and say "Bido, I understand your passion but you have to package it differently", or 'Bido, you must decide if you will stay or you will go because the cost is too much even though I know leaving is not what you want to do." In those moments my leaders taught me that change wasn't defeat. It was one of the most important things I ever learned. Sometimes we hold on too long and it costs us who we are as human beings.

The Person vs The Process is about the steps you take to lead, to know, to understand, to change, to empower and to impact the lives of others by not dismissing the process of leading. Above all may your leadership open doors for others to lead.

In the end I AM…

"tryin' to give you a million dollars worth of game for $9.99."

- Jay-z

ABOUT THE AUTHOR

JACQUELEEN M. BIDO, EDD

A Newark, New Jersey native, Dr. Jacqueleen Bido earned her Doctorate from Seton Hall University in Educational Leadership, Management, and Policy. Dr. Bido served in Operation Iraqi Freedom and Operation Enduring Freedom during her time in the US Navy as an Information Systems Tech. As a former District Administrator for Parent and Family Engagement in the Orange County Public Schools Title I Department she coached and trained 73 Parent Engagement Liaisons and schools in implementing successful communication strategies and systems for engaging parents, families, and the community. While in the Orange County Public Schools Minority Achievement Office she focused on Males of Color, My Brother's Keeper and Find Your Voice Initiatives to impact academic and social-emotional disparities. She is the founder of Elevate Newark and BIDOISM, LLC., which are consulting companies created to empower and help people, their organizations, and the communities they serve to invoke social change. She continues to expand her mission through business consultation, program development, and grant writing to support local and national initiatives.As community collaborator and dynamic trainer she seeks to engage all stakeholders in a "Strategy for Peace of Mind."She is a mother to five beautiful children, who have been her greatest achievement because their mere existence proves the importance of the work she does to make the world a better place for them and all to live.

BIDOISM

A STRATEGY
FOR
PEACE OF MIND

www.ingramcontent.com/pod-product-compliance
Lightning Source LLC
Chambersburg PA
CBHW081633040426
42449CB00014B/3286